Sarah B. Estabrook

The appetizer

A thoroughly reliable cook book

Sarah B. Estabrook

The appetizer
A thoroughly reliable cook book

ISBN/EAN: 9783744786089

Printed in Europe, USA, Canada, Australia, Japan

Cover: Foto ©Lupo / pixelio.de

More available books at **www.hansebooks.com**

--THE APPETIZER--

A THOROUGHLY RELIABLE

COOK BOOK:

*Every recipe having been tested
by experienced Cooks.* . . .

WORCESTER:
Press of Lucius P. Goddard, 425 Main Street.
1893.

BOSTON STORE.

A Good Cook

Ought to have a good variety of dishes, pots and pans and mixing things, to do her cooking with.

In these days of labor saving contrivances, it is a pity that any woman should be without all the utensils that make cooking both easy and pleasant.

No woman would be without any of the things she needs in this line, if she fully realized for how little money they can be bought.

Not everyone knows that we carry a large stock of such articles, yet such is the case. Those who do know it know also that we sell kitchen things, as we do all other goods, at the lowest of low prices.

Our large transactions make it possible for us to do this, since through our connection with the Syndicate Trading Company of New York we are able to purchase goods of all kinds at lower rates than can be done by dealers who have not the advantage of such connection.

For all kitchen articles, then, such as mixing bowls, and spoons, egg beaters, flour sieves, chopping bowls, trays and knives, pie plates, pudding dishes, bread and cake tins, tea kettles, tea pots, roasting pans, etc., etc., visit our kitchen furnishings department, in our basement.

You will find the assortment the large and best, and the prices the lowest in this region.

Denholm & McKay Co.

WORCESTER, MASS.

Main Street, opposite Park Street.

SOUPS.

Clam Chowder.

One quart clams, salt and pepper to taste, one quart sliced potatoes, 2 small onions, 8 crackers, 1 quart water, 1 quart milk. Wash clams thoroughly in the quart of water and strain the liquid through a muslin. Boil potatoes in this until cooked. Slice onions and fry in butter until a golden brown, and add to the potatoes while they are cooking. Add the milk and spread over the top the crackers which have previously been split and softened in cold salted water, placing a piece of butter size of a walnut on each half. Cook slowly twenty minutes. Then add the clams and boil up once.

Potato Soup.

Pare 6 potatoes and let them simmer in a pint of water with 1 onion sliced. When thoroughly cooked strain through a sieve and add a pint of milk; salt to taste. When hot stir in 1 egg well beaten. Serve immediately.

Corn Chowder.

Fry 2 or 3 slices fat salt pork (one onion if you wish). Strain into a kettle; add one quart sliced potatoes and 1 quart boiling water. Cook till potatoes are done, add one quart hot milk, 1 can of corn (or one quart grated fresh corn), and bring to a boil. Add three tablespoonfuls butter, salt and pepper.

Mock Bisque Soup.

1 quart can tomatoes, 3 pints milk, 1 large table spoonful flour, butter the size of an egg, pepper and salt to taste, 1 scant teaspoonful soda. Put the tomato on to stew, and the milk in a double kettle to boil, reserving however half a cupful to mix with flour. Mix the flour smoothly with this cold milk, stir into the boiling milk, and cook ten minutes. To the tomato add the soda; stir well and rub through a strainer that is fine enough to keep back the seeds. Add butter, salt and pepper to the milk, and then the tomato. Serve immediately. If half the rule is made, stir the tomato well in the can before dividing, as the liquid portion is the more acid.

Potato Soup.

1 quart milk, 6 large potatoes, one stalk celery, 1 onion and one table spoonful butter. Put milk to boil with onion and

celery. Pare potatoes and boil thirty minutes. Turn off the water, and mash fine and light. Add boiling milk, and butter, and pepper and salt to taste. Rub through a strainer and serve immediately. A cupful of whipped cream, added when in the tureen, is a great improvement. This soup must not be allowed to stand, not even if kept hot. Served as soon as ready, it is excellent.

FISH.

Fish a la Creme.

4 pounds of fish (haddock preferred). 1 pint cream sauce, 1 cup cracker crumbs, moistened in $\frac{1}{3}$ of a cup of melted butter. Clean the fish, cook in boiling salted water (or steam) till the flesh separates. When cool remove the skin and bones, and pick apart in flakes. Make a rich white sauce. Put a layer of fish in a dish suitable for serving. Cover with the sauce, letting the fish soak up all it will; then arrange another layer of fish and sauce until all is used. Spread the moistened crumbs over the top, set in the oven and bake till the crumbs are brown.

White Sauce for Fish.

1 pint milk, 2 tablespoonfuls butter, 2 heaping tablespoonfuls flour, salt and pepper.

Heat the milk over hot water. Put the butter in a granite saucepan and stir until it melts and bubbles. Add the dry flour, and stir quickly till well mixed. Add the milk slowly, and stir vigorously till well mixed and perfectly smooth.

Cusk.

Mince 2 lbs. salt codfish; 1 quart cream or rich milk. Mix 4 tablespoonfuls corn starch with $\frac{1}{2}$ cup butter, and stir into the boiling milk. Add the juice of a small onion (if desired), a little parsley, salt and pepper. Cover with buttered crumbs, and bake till brown.

Fish Hash.

The same mixture as above, cooked in a little salt pork fat till brown, and turned out like an omelet.

Fish Souffle.

Prepare as above; add two tablespoonfuls of cream and two beaten eggs. Bake in a buttered dish.

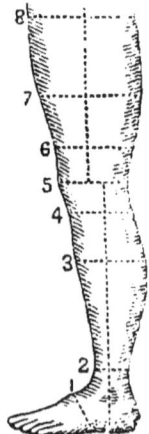

Salt Fish Balls.

1 cup raw salt fish, 2 cups potato, 1 teaspoonful butter, 1 egg well beaten, salt.

Pick the fish in pieces and free from bones. Cut the potatoes in small pieces. Boil together, till potatoes are soft. Drain off all the water; mash and beat the fish and potatoes until very light. Add the butter, salt, and a little pepper. When slightly cool add the egg. Shape in a tablespoon without smoothing much, slip them off into a basket, and fry in *smoking hot* lard or cottolene (I prefer the latter) one minute. Fry only five or six at a time, as more will cool the fat. The fat should be hot enough to brown a piece of bread while you count forty.

MEATS.

Meat Souffle.

1 pint cooked meat finely chopped, 1 pint cream sauce, 4 eggs, 1 teaspoonful chopped parsley, 1 teaspoonful onion juice, salt and pepper to taste. Stir meat and seasoning into the boiling sauce; cook two minutes, add the yolks of the eggs well beaten, and set away to cool. When cold, add whites beaten to a stiff froth. Bake in a buttered dish half an hour. Serve immediately.

Croquettes.

1 solid pint chopped chicken or mixed meats, 1 tablespoonful salt (scant), ½ teaspoonful celery salt, 1 salt-spoonful pepper (black or white), 1 teaspoonful onion juice, 1 tablespoonful lemon juice, 1 table spoonful chopped parsley, 1 egg, 1 pint cream sauce

For the sauce scald 1 pint milk, cream or stock. If milk is used add 2 tablespoonfuls butter, if cream or stock, 1. Cook the butter and 2 heaping tablespoonfuls flour until smooth; add the boiling liquid slowly. Stir constantly until smooth and of the consistency of paste. Mix with the seasoned meat. When cold, shape, roll in fine bread crumbs, and fry in a wire basket in boiling fat. They will fry better if shaped and rolled several hours before frying. The fat should be hot enough to brown a piece of bread while counting forty.

Beef-steak Loaf.

4 lbs. chopped raw beef (the round is best), 8 pounded crackers, 1 cup sweet milk, piece of butter the size of an egg,

3 teaspoonfuls salt, 1 teaspoonful pepper, 4 well beaten eggs. Mix well and bake two hours.

Scalloped Chicken.

Take equal parts of cold roast or boiled chicken, cold rice and tomato sauce. Put in layers in a shallow dish. Cover with buttered crumbs and bake till done.

SALADS, Etc.

Potato Salad.

Cut cold boiled potatoes in dice shape. Scrape or cut very fine a very small onion, and mix thoroughly with the potato. Beat with an egg beater 6 tablespoonfuls sweet cream, 4 tablespoonfuls vinegar; salt and pepper. Pour over the potato.

Potato a la Duchesse.

Take 5 middle-sized potatoes (cold boiled), grate and mix with them 5 dessert-spoonfuls flour, adding to the mixture 2 well beaten eggs and a jill of milk; salt. Mix thoroughly, make into balls, and drop into hot fat, and fry a light brown.

Salad Dressing.

1 cup cream, 1 cup butter, 4 eggs, 1 pint vinegar, 1 large spoonful each of salt and mustard, $\frac{1}{2}$ cup sugar, $\frac{1}{2}$ teaspoonful cayenne. Cook like soft custard.

Cream Salad Dressing.

2 eggs, 3 tablespoonfuls vinegar, juice of half a lemon, 1 tablespoonful cream, 1 teaspoonful sugar, $\frac{1}{4}$ teaspoonful salt, $\frac{1}{4}$ teaspoonful mustard, 1 tablespoonful butter. Beat the eggs well. Add the sugar, salt, mustard, then the vinegar and lemon juice, butter and cream. Place bowl in basin of boiling water, and stir until about the thickness of rich cream.

Salad Dressing.

1 cup cream, 1 cup vinegar, 3 eggs, 1 tablespoonful each of sugar and butter, $\frac{1}{2}$ tablespoonful salt, and scant tablespoonful mustard, pepper. Mix thoroughly, and boil till thick like custard.

Cream Salad Dressing.

1 cup of cream, 1 cup of butter, 5 eggs, 1 teaspoonful of salt, 1 teaspoonful of dry mustard, $\frac{1}{4}$ teaspoonful of red pepper, $\frac{1}{2}$ cup of sugar (small), a small half pint of vinegar. Put the cream on to boil in a double kettle, then beat together butter,

1873 — 1893

WM. HYLAND,

Manufacturer and Dealer in

Mattresses, Springs, Comforters,

HUSK, COTTON, WOOL,

And everything in the **BEDDING** Line.

Feather Beds Renovated,

Hair Mattresses made over,

Called for and returned the same day.

Mr. H. being the leading Manufacturer

in the country, satisfaction can be guaranteed in all cases. He produces an average of

250 Mattresses per day.

There can be no delay in the work, as he has 40 steady men at work the year round.

eggs, sugar and mustard, then stir this mixture into the boiling cream, and stir constantly until it thickens, then remove from the fire and turn in the vinegar, which should be heating meanwhile, and give it a good beating for a minute. Use a wooden spoon.

Egg Salad.

Boil a dozen eggs, and cut the whites in halves. Mix with the yolks 1 teaspoonful minced ham, small piece of butter, teaspoonful each of salt, sugar and celery seed, 4 tablespoonfuls vinegar. Fill whites of eggs with the mixture.

Scalloped Potatoes.

Slice raw potatoes thin as for chips. Place in cooking dish, in layers, with salt, butter, pepper and a little onion if desired. Nearly cover with milk. Bake until potatoes are soft.

EGGS.

Stuffed Eggs.

Boil 6 eggs 20 minutes. Mash the yolks and add one teaspoonful soft butter, and half the quantity of minced chicken, lamb or veal. Season with salt, pepper and chopped parsley. Fill the whites with the mixture, and press the two halves together. Spread the remainder of the yolk mixture on a baking dish, and place the eggs on it. Cover with a thin white sauce, or chicken or veal gravy. Sprinkle buttered crumbs over the whole, and bake till the crumbs are a delicate brown.

Scrambled Eggs with Ham.

Dip slices of toast in hot salted water. Butter slightly, and spread with finely chopped ham. Scramble eggs in the proportion of 2 eggs and butter size of half an egg, to one cup milk.

Eggs a la Golden-rod.

Boil three eggs hard. Pour a cupful of white sauce over the chopped whites. Press the yolks through a sieve over the sauce, season with salt and pepper.

Egg Omelet.

6 eggs; divide the yolks from whites; beat yolks thoroughly, add 1 tablespoonful cornstarch dissolved in a little milk, add 1 coffee cup rich milk slowly, salt. Beat the whites very stiff, salting them first; stir in last thing lightly. Pour all in hot buttered spider. Do not turn.

Baked Omelet.

Boil ½ pint of milk; beat 6 eggs very light, yolks and whites separately. Put ½ teaspoonful of salt and a piece of butter half as large as an egg into the boiling milk, and stir it into the beaten yolks. Place the whites in a deep dish, and pour the custard over it. Bake ten minutes in a quick oven. It should be a delicious brown. Eat hot.

RELISHES.

Chow-Chow.

1 large red cabbage, 1 large cauliflower, 2 quarts each very small string beans, small tomatoes (green), cucumbers, and silverskin onions. Quarter the cabbage and remove the core, then shave in thin slices; break the cauliflower into flowerets, but leave the others whole. Mix thoroughly, add 1 pint fine salt, and let stand over night. In the morning rinse in cold water and drain. Then add 1 oz. celery seed, 1 oz. white mustard seed, and 1 small box ground mustard. Cover well with vinegar and boil twenty minutes or half an hour. Mix ¼ lb. granulated sugar and 1 tablespoonful turmeric, and stir in thoroughly while the mixture is cooling.

Higdum.

Chop fine green tomatoes, salt thoroughly and let remain over night. Pour off the juice, and to each gallon of tomatoes add 2 quarts of chopped cabbage, 3 onions chopped fine, 3 lbs. sugar (brown preferred), 2 quarts vinegar, 1 teaspoonful each of cloves, cinnamon and whole mustard, a little pepper, and 1 tablespoonful of celery seed. This is not cooked, but all ingredients added cold.

Pickled Fruit.

10 pounds fruit, 3 lbs. sugar, 1 pint vinegar, 1 tablespoonful cloves, a few pieces cinnamon bark, 1 cup water, and cook until soft. Put all in the kettle at the same time.

Pepper Hash.

Chop 1 large sized white cabbage and 8 peppers fine, 4 green and 4 red tomatoes, small cup salt. Mix well and let stand 24 hours, then drain and add 5 cents' worth mustard seed, 1 tablespoonful each ground cloves and cinnamon. Mix well and cover with 3 pints scalded vinegar.

Chili Sauce.

10 tomatoes, 4 green peppers, 3 onions, peppers and onions chopped fine, 2 cups sugar, 3 cups vinegar, 1 tablespoonful salt, ½ teaspoonful all kinds of spice. Cook two hours.

Chili Sauce.

12 large ripe tomatoes, 2 green peppers, 2 chopped onions, 1 tablespoonful sugar, 1 tablespoonful salt, 2 cups vinegar, 1 teaspoonful each of ginger, cloves, cinnamon, allspice, nutmeg. Boil half an hour.

French Mustard.

4 ounces Colburn's mustard, 1 ounce powdered sugar, teaspoonful salt. Rub well together with the hand. Boil ½ pint good vinegar. Pour about half the vinegar (boiling) on the ingredients in the bowl, and stir quickly and thoroughly until all the lumps are out. Add enough boiling vinegar to reduce the mixture to a smooth paste, just thick enough to run slowly off the spoon. Keep in a corked bottle in a cool place and let stand 24 hours before using.

Pickled Tomatoes.

8 quarts green tomatoes, 4 onions, 2 green peppers; slice, salt, and let them stand over night. In the morning add 1 pound brown sugar, and ½ ounce each of whole cloves, allspice, and mustard seed. Cook till tender.

Spiced Currants.

5 lbs. currants, 4 lbs. sugar, 2 tablespoonfuls each of clove, allspice and cinnamon, 1 pt. vinegar. Simmer 2 hours.

Grape Ketchup.

5 lbs. grapes (wild ones are very nice for this), 2½ lbs. sugar, 1 pint vinegar, 1 tablespoonful each of cinnamon, clove, allspice, and pepper, ½ tablespoonful of salt. Boil the grapes with water to nearly cover them, and put through a colander. Add spices, and boil until a little thick.

Sweet Tomato Pickle—very nice.

1 peck of green tomatoes and 6 large onions sliced or chopped. Sprinkle with 1 cupful of salt and let stand over night. In the morning drain. Add to the tomatoes 2 quarts of water, and 1 quart of vinegar; boil 15 minutes, then drain, and throw this vinegar and water away. Add to the pickle 2 pounds of sugar, 2 qts. of vinegar, 2 tablespoonfuls each of cinnamon, allspice, clove, ginger, mustard, and 1 teaspoonful cayenne. Boil till soft.

Dr. D. FRANCIS ESTABROOK,

DENTIST

First - Class Work

.·. FOR .·.

Reasonable Prices.

Plate Work a Specialty.

20 Pearl Street,

Y. M. C. A. BUILDING,   OPPOSITE POST OFFICE.

Chili Sauce.

18 large tomatoes, 4 green peppers, 2 onions, all chopped fine. 2 tablespoonfuls salt, 2 cupfuls sugar, 2 cupfuls vinegar. Boil all together.

Pickles.

1 peck green tomatoes sliced, 1 doz. onions sliced, 1 dozen small cucumbers or large ones sliced, 1 quart string beans, 2 cauliflowers cut up. Salt all over night. In the morning drain off the liquor, and add 4 ears of green corn shelled, 2 heads of celery, ½ lb. brown sugar, ¼ lb. white mustard seed, ½ cup grated horse radish, 1 tablespoonful ground cloves, enough vinegar to cover all. Boil half an hour. Lastly, add ⅓ lb. English mustard mixed with cold vinegar, stir in and let it *just come to a boil.*

Chopped Sweet Pickle.

4 quarts of green chopped tomatoes, add ½ cup fine salt, and let it stand over night. Drain thoroughly, add 1 quart chopped cabbage, 1 pint chopped onions, 3 spoonfuls whole cloves, 4 spoonfuls ground cassia, 1 spoonful ground black pepper, 3 spoonfuls ground mustard, 2 spoonfuls ginger, 1 lb. sugar, 1 quart good cider vinegar. Boil until tender, but not too soft.

Grape Catsup.

Boil the grapes and sift, then to 5 lbs. of the pulp add 2½ lbs. sugar, 1 pint vinegar, cinnamon, cloves, allspice and pepper each 1 teaspoonful, ½ tablespoonful salt. Boil until the proper thickness.

Green Tomato Preserve.

1 peck green tomatoes sliced and steamed (or cooked in clear water) until you can pierce with a straw. Drain off water and weigh, 1 lb. of sugar to 1 lb. of tomatoes, not quite so sweet if not desired, 7 lemons, 1 oz. white ginger root. Simmer 3 or 4 hours.

Tomatoes a la Creme.

Peel and slice tomatoes, season with salt and pepper, dip in flour and fry in butter. Serve with cream sauce.

MUFFINS, GEMS, BREADS, Etc.

Muffins.

1 egg, 1 tablespoonful butter, 1 cup sugar, ½ cup milk, ½ teaspoonful soda, 1 teaspoonful cream of tartar, flour enough to make a good batter. Bake quickly.

Graham Bread.

1 pint milk scalded, 2 teaspoonfuls salt, ¾ yeast cake, flour enough for thick batter. When the batter is· light, add 1 cup cold milk, with ¾ teaspoonful saleratus, large half cup sugar, and graham or Arlington meal to make a soft dough Put in the pans and let it rise until light. Then bake. If the batter is made in the morning, part of the dough can be baked in muffin-pans for tea. This rule makes 12 large muffins and a loaf of bread. Do not mix the muffins quite as stiff as the bread.

Graham Muffins.

1½ cups white flour, 1½ cups graham flour, ½ cup molasses, 1 teaspoonful saleratus, 2 teaspoonfuls cream of tartar, 1½ cups milk, salt.

Sour Milk Muffins.

1 cup flour, 1 cup meal, 1 cup sour milk, ½ cup molasses, 1 teaspoonful saleratus, salt.

Brown Bread.

3 cups thick sour milk, 2 cups Indian meal, 2 cups rye meal, 1 cup molasses, 2 even teaspoonfuls saleratus. Steam 3 hours.

Breakfast Muffins.

1 cup white flour, ½ cup graham flour, 1 teaspoonful cream of tartar, ½ teaspoonful saleratus, 2 tablespoonfuls sugar, 2 table-spoonfuls melted butter, 1 egg, cup milk. Bake in hot gem pans.'

Pop-Overs.

1 cup flour, 1 cup milk, 1 egg, pinch saleratus, salt. Bake quickly in hot pans.

Johnny Cake.

1 cup Indian meal, ½ cup flour, ½ cup molasses, ½ teaspoonful salt, ½ teaspoonful saleratus, 1 cup sour milk.

German Puffs.

6 eggs, leaving out the whites of three for sauce, 6 table-spoonfuls flour, 1 tablespoonful melted butter, 1 pint milk. Bake in gem pans in a quick oven. Place on a platter, and pour over them the following sauce: 1 large cup sugar and the juice of 4 or 5 oranges added to the whites of 3 eggs, beaten stiff.

Corn Cake.

2 eggs, ½ cup sugar, 2 teaspoonfuls cream of tartar, ½ tea-spoonful saleratus, 1 cup milk, 1 tablespoonful melted butter. Mix thin enough to run with half Indian meal and half flour.

DESSERTS.

Pudding Sauce.

2 eggs, 1 cup sugar, 3 tablespoonfuls cream. Beat yolks and sugar together, add cream, hot, add beaten whites of eggs. Flavor.

Steamed Graham Pudding.

1 cup molasses, ½ cup warm water, 1 cup raisins chopped, piece of butter the size of a walnut, salt, a little wheat flour, 1 teaspoonful soda. Mix the Graham flour to the consistency of molasses gingerbread, and steam two or three hours.

Fruit Jellies.

Make any nice lemon jelly, adding either strawberries mashed with plenty of sugar, or sliced peaches sweetened. Use the same amount of lemon as for the plain jelly. These jellies are very nice served cold with cream.

Pineapple Sherbet.

To 1 can pineapple allow 1 pint sugar and one heaping table-spoonful gelatine Chop the pineapple very fine, add the juice of fruit and the sugar. Soak the gelatine in cold water until dissolved, then add ½ cup hot water, and mix with pineapple. Serve cold.

Caramel Custard.

1½ cups sugar, 6 eggs, 1 quart milk, salt. Melt the sugar in a spider over a hot fire. Pour it in the scalding milk. Add the beaten yolks of eggs, then the salt, and vanilla flavoring. Use whites of eggs for frosting. Bake same as ordinary custard.

Plain Cup Custard.

1 quart scalded milk, 4 eggs beaten, 4 tablespoonfuls sugar, salt. Bake in pan half filled with hot water.

Tapioca Pudding.

Soak for an hour ½ cup pearl tapioca in ⅔ cup of cold water. Scald this mixture (until the tapioca swells) in a pint of milk; then add it to the following conglomeration: ½ cup sugar con-taining a small pinch of cinnamon, a little salt, 2 eggs, first melting in the milk a small piece of butter. Bake in a buttered dish about ¾ of an hour.

Tapioca Cream.

Soak 4 tablespoonfuls tapioca over night. To 1 quart boiling milk add ⅔ cup of sugar, yolks of three eggs, a little salt. Boil till consistency of a custard. Use whites of eggs for frosting.

Spanish Cream.

1½ pints of milk, ½ box gelatine. Mix and let it remain an hour. Add the yolks of 3 eggs, and two small cups of sugar. Scald as thick as soft custard, then stir in the whites of the eggs beaten to a stiff froth. Flavor to taste. Pour in a mold and cool gradually.

Apricot Cream.

Take a pint of preserved apricots, turn out into a saucepan, add 2 ounces of sugar, let them boil for a quarter of an hour, and pass them through a strainer. Dissolve ¼ box of gelatine in a little milk, whip to a froth a pint of cream. Mix the gelatine with the apricot pulp, then quickly work into it the cream. Pour the mixture into a mold and put it on the ice to set. When wanted, dip the mold in hot water and turn out the cream. Peaches can be used the same way.

Roman Cream.

½ box of gelatine, 6 eggs, 8 tablespoonfuls sugar, 1 quart milk. Put the gelatine and milk on to boil. Beat the yolks of the eggs and sugar together, and stir in. Flavor to taste. When a little cool stir in the whites beaten to a stiff froth.

Caramel Custard.

1 quart of milk, 1 cup sugar, 3 eggs, pinch of salt. Put milk on to scald, brown the sugar in a saucepan and add to the milk; when dissolved, add the beaten eggs, and bake like any custard.

Strawberry Pudding.

Yolks of 2 eggs, 1 cup sugar, 1 cup milk, 2 cups flour, 1 teaspoonful yeast powder. While it is baking beat the whites of the eggs as for frosting, adding powdered sugar until quite stiff. Have ready one quart of strawberries (less will do), and mash them thoroughly in a bowl. When the pudding is ready to serve stir the berries into the frosting and serve as a sauce for the pudding.

Chocolate Custard.

Into 2 cups of boiling milk stir the yolks of two eggs beaten with ½ cup sugar, 1 large tablespoonful of corn starch and a pinch of salt. Stir until it thickens, and flavor with vanilla. When cold cover this with frosting: Beat the whites of 2 eggs to a stiff froth, add ¼ cup sugar, and 1 tablespoonful of grated chocolate.

Tapioca Pudding.

2 tablespoonfuls tapioca soaked over night. Drain off water and add 1 pint of milk, the yolks of 2 eggs. Boil in double

boiler, sweeten and flavor to taste; place in oven, after spreading on frosting made of whites of the eggs.

Cracker Pudding.

3 crackers rolled fine, yolks of 2 eggs, 1 pint of milk, $\frac{3}{3}$ cup of raisins, $\frac{2}{3}$ cup sugar, salt and nutmeg. Bake one hour. Beat whites of eggs with 1 tablespoonful sugar, spread on top and brown.

Spanish Cream.

3 pints of milk poured on 1 ounce of gelatine to soak one hour; 6 eggs, 8 tablespoonfuls sugar. Beat sugar and yolks together, and pour into the milk while boiling; then pour the mixture on the whites of the eggs which have previously been beaten. Flavor with vanilla. Put it in a mold when cold. Serve with cream.

Baked Rice Pudding.

Boil $\frac{1}{2}$ cup of rice in 1 pint of water 30 minutes, add 1 quart milk and boil 30 minutes. Beat together 3 eggs, 1 cup sugar, 2 teaspoonfuls salt, a little lemon or nutmeg, and stir into the rice. Put in a pudding dish and bake 30 minutes.

Coffee Jelly.

1 pint sugar, 1 pint strong coffee, $1\frac{1}{2}$ pints boiling water, $\frac{1}{2}$ pint cold water, 1 box gelatine. Soak the gelatine two hours in cold water. Pour the boiling water on it, and when it is dissolved add the sugar and coffee. Strain, turn into molds and set away to harden. This is to be served with sugar and cream.

Lemon Pudding.

9 tablespoonfuls grated apple, 1 lemon (grated), peel and pulp, $\frac{1}{2}$ cup butter, $\frac{1}{2}$ pint milk, 2 cups sugar, 3 eggs. Beat butter, sugar and eggs to a cream, then add the apple and milk. Line a pudding dish with rich crust, bake half an hour. A meringue of whites of 3 eggs and 3 tablespoonfuls sugar may be added if liked.

Pudding Sauce.

(Nice for suet and other steamed puddings.)

Mix 1 teaspoonful corn starch with two cups granulated sugar. Pour over this 1 cup hot water, and let it boil. Slice into the boiling syrup 2 or 3 tart apples in very thin bits, and let the whole boil until the apple is clear and semi-transparent. Pour this on to 2 tablespoonfuls (good measure) butter, creamed. Flavor slightly with vanilla. When served the sauce should be of the consistency of syrup.

NEW YORK BIRD STORE,

DEALERS IN

SINGING AND TALKING BIRDS,

Cages and Food

In great variety.

C. C. Webster & Co.

268

MAIN STREET,

Worcester, Mass.

MISS C. KENNARD,

Ladies' Hair Dressing Parlors,

CHILDREN'S HAIR CUTTING

And all kinds of

HAIR WORK MADE TO ORDER.

WIG-MAKING A SPECIALTY.

387 Main St., Worcester, Mass.

GROUT'S BLOCK.

FACIAL MASSAGE TREATMENT GIVEN.

Ginger Cream.

Soak ½ box of gelatine in ½ cup cold water 20 minutes. Boil 1 pint milk, add beaten yolks of 4 eggs, ½ cup sugar, ¼ teaspoonful salt. Cook until thick like custard; add gelatine, strain into a pan and set on ice. Add ⅓ cup ginger syrup, ¼ pound ginger cut in small pieces. When thick add 1 pint cream whipped. Pour in a mold.

Fuller Pudding.

1 cup molasses, 1 cup sweet milk, 1 egg, butter the size of an egg, clove and cinnamon, 1 cup stoned raisins, 1 teaspoonful soda, 2 teaspoonfuls cream of tartar, flour as for soft ginger-bread. Steam three hours. Use cold sauce.

Custard Souffle.

2 scant tablespoonfuls butter, 2 tablespoonfuls flour, 2 tablespoonfuls sugar, 1 cupful milk, 4 eggs. Let the milk come to a boil. Beat the flour and butter together; add them to the boiling milk gradually, and cook eight minutes, stirring often. Beat sugar and yolks of eggs and add to the cooked mixture and set away to cool. When cool beat whites to a stiff froth and add to the mixture. Bake in a buttered dish for twenty minutes in a moderate oven. Serve *immediately*.

Sauce for Souffle.

Whites of 2 eggs beaten to a stiff froth. Add 1 coffee-cupful sugar, beat well. Then add 1 tumblerful orange juice. Any other fruit juice or a box of strawberries, mashed, may be substituted for the oranges.

Prune Souffle.

½ lb. prunes stewed and chopped fine. Whites of 6 eggs beaten to a stiff froth; add 12 tablespoonfuls powdered sugar, and beat well, then whip in lightly the prunes. Bake in buttered dish for ten or fifteen minutes in a moderate oven. Serve with cream *immediately*.

Boiled Indian Pudding.

1 pint milk, 1 egg, 1½ tablespoonfuls molasses; mix as hard as pancakes, with fine meal, salt. Boil 5 hours. Sauce to your taste.

Baked Indian Pudding.

1 quart milk, scald; mix 1 full cup meal with cold milk, then pour it on the scalding milk, stirring it, and sweeten it with molasses to taste, allspice and salt, and ½ cup of cold milk, when putting it in the oven.

Hog Pudding.

3 quarts Indian meal, 1 pint rye meal, 1½ pints of molasses, 1 pound lard, ½ pound beef suet, allspice and raisins. Scald with hot milk half the meal, then mix with cold milk, put them in boiling water, and boil two hours.

Orange Short Cake.

1 egg, 1 tablespoonful butter, 3 cups flour, 1 cup milk, 1 teaspoonful cream of tartar, ½ teaspoonful soda, 2 tablespoonfuls sugar; beat sugar and butter to a cream.

Caramel Ice Cream.

1½ pints milk, 2 eggs, 1 coffee-cup sugar, 1 teaspoonful gelatine, 1 pint cream, 1 tablespoonful vanilla. Scald the milk; melt the sugar over a hot fire until the lumps are all out, pour into the milk and let it dissolve. Pour this on to the beaten eggs and the gelatine which has been soaked in cold water. Cook until slightly thickened, and let it stand over night. Before freezing add 1 pint of cream and flavoring. Less cream can be used with good results.

Thanksgiving Plum Pudding.

Cut a loaf of baker's bread; boil 1 quart of milk, and pour on to it while hot, cover and let it stand until cool. Then add ½ lb. currants, ½ lb. raisins, stoned and cut, ¼ lb. citron cut fine, 1 nutmeg, 1 tablespoonful mace and cinnamon mixed, ½ lb. butter cut in small pieces, ½ lb sugar, 4 eggs well beaten. Dredge the fruit with flour to prevent sinking. Bake two hours.

Apple Snow Pudding.

Steam till tender 6 good sized apples. When cold, add a cup of sugar and the whites of 2 eggs beaten to a stiff froth. Beat the yolks with ½ cup of sugar and a cup of milk or cream, and use as a sauce.

Mountain Dew Pudding.

3 crackers pounded or rolled fine. 1 pint of milk, yolks of two eggs, and a little salt. Bake half an hour. Beat the whites of the two eggs to a stiff froth, add 1 cup of sugar, a pinch of salt, and flavor with lemon. Pour over the pudding, and set in the oven to brown slightly.

Raisin Pudding.

1 quart milk, ⅔ cup raisins, ⅔ cup sugar, 1 heaping tablespoonful rice, piece of butter size of a egg. Bake four hours in a slow oven. Stir often.

School of English Speech,

COLONIAL HALL BUILDING,   WORCESTER, MASS.

SIXTH YEAR BEGAN

Tuesday, October 3, 1893.

DIRECTORS:

MRS. JOHN C. CUTTER,   MRS. WILLIAM E. BOWEN.

Class and Private Instruction in

Reading, Æsthetic Culture (Delsarte),
    Pantomimic Action,
        Abdominal Breathing Exercises,
            Pronunciation, Shakespeare Study,
                History, Literature, and Letter Writing.

The excellent work of the school in reading and gesture was fully shown at the closing recitals of last June. These recitals received the highest praise from the press as well as from the large audiences that were present at every recital. Next June Shakespeare's Midsummer Night's Dream will be given with Mendelssohn's music, scenery, appropriate costumes, etc. Pupils of the school will have the benefit of the preparatory drills.

Entertainment.

The School is prepared to supply the best local talent in Reading, Greek Tableaux, Pantomime, etc., for

CHURCH, LODGE AND PARLOR ENTERTAINMENTS.

For terms and fuller particulars apply to

The School of English Speech,

34 FRONT STREET,

WORCESTER, MASS,

Italian Cream

Whip a pint of cream, add ½ box of gelatine dissolved in ½ pint of cold water, 1 teaspoonful vanilla, 1½ cups sugar, ½ gill of wine. Beat well and pour into mold.

Snowball Pudding.

Take 1 pint boiling water, put in a kettle, then take 3 table-spoonfuls of corn starch, ½ cup of sugar, a little salt. Use a little cold water to dissolve it, then stir in the boiling water. Have ready the whites of 2 eggs beaten to a froth, and when the other is cooked stir in the whites. Take from the fire and flavor, put in cups to cool. Take yolks of the eggs for cream, which is made the same as any snow pudding.

Judge Peter's Pudding.

½ box gelatine, ½ pint cold water, ½ pint boiling water, 2 cups sugar, juice of two lemons, 6 dates, 4 figs, 2 banannas, 6 almonds blanched. Dissolve gelatine in cold water, add the boiling water and sugar. When jelly is cool, before it has hardened, put in the fruit which has been cut in small pieces, stir and put in mold. Should be kept over night. Nice if served with cream or soft custard.

Emily Pudding.

Fill a dish half full of apples cored and sliced. Mix 1 cup molasses, 1 teaspoonful soda, a little salt, and flour enough to make it thick as gingerbread. Pour this over the apples and bake slowly one hour. Serve hot with whipped cream or sauce

Cornucopia.

3 eggs, 1 cup sugar, 1 cup flour, 2 tablespoonfuls cold water. Use 1 tablespoonful of the mixture for each round tin in which they are baked. While hot lap edges together to form cornu-copia, hold in shape until cool. Fill with whipped cream or jelly.

Judge Peter.

¾ box of gelatine, 2 oranges, 2 lemons, 6 figs, 9 dates. 10 al-monds, 5 English walnuts. Dissolve gelatine in 1 pint cold water for 1 hour. add ½ pint of boiling water, the juice of lemons and 1 orange, and 2 cups sugar. Let it stand until it begins to thicken. Cut the fruit, nuts, and other orange in small pieces, mix well with the jelly, and pour into molds. Serve with whipped cream.

Rice Pudding.

1 quart scalded milk, ⅔ cup stoned raisins, ⅔ cup sugar, butter, size of an egg, heaping tablespoonful raw rice. Bake four hours in a slow oven.

DAVIS ART CO.

18 PEARL ST.   Opposite Post Office.

Etchings AND Engravings.

•❈•

⚬ Picture Framing ⚬

J. B CROCKER.

Canterbury Street Pharmacy.

101 Canterbury Street, corner of Grand,

SOUTH WORCESTER,

Drugs, Medicines, Chemicals,

FINE TOILET SOAPS, BRUSHES, COMBS, ETC.

—✳—❀—

Perfumery, and Fancy Toilet Articles,

In great variety.

PHYSICIAN'S PRESCRIPTIONS

Carefully Compounded by a Competent Pharmacist.

Circassian Pudding.

Boil 6 tablespoonfuls dried bread crumbs in 1 pint of milk. Stir in the yolks of 3 eggs beaten with 6 tablespoonfuls of sugar and a piece of butter size of an English walnut. Take from the fire and stir in gradually the beaten whites of 3 eggs. When the mixture is cool, pour into a buttered dish, and bake slowly. Flavor with a few drops of vanilla.

Suet Pudding.

1 cup chopped suet, 1 cup molasses, 1 cup milk, 3 cups flour, 1 cup chopped raisins, 1 teaspoonful saleratus. Steam 3 hours.

Baked Blueberry Pudding.

Mix 1 cup of sugar with a piece of butter the size of a large egg, 1 cup of milk, 1 teaspoonful cream of tartar, $\frac{1}{2}$ teaspoonful saleratus, 2 cups flour, 1 coffee cup of blueberries well sprinkled with flour. *Sauce.*— $\frac{1}{3}$ cup of butter, beaten light, $\frac{2}{3}$ of a cup of sugar, and the yolk of 1 egg. Mix well, and pour on it one cup of boiling water. When it cooks a little, add the beaten white of the egg, stirring in a spoonful at a time.

Bird's Nest Pudding.

Pare and core 6 apples. Place in an earthen dish and fill the holes with sugar. Make a batter of 1 pint of milk, 2 table-spoonfuls of flour, and 3 eggs. Pour this over the apples, and bake till the fruit is soft. Serve with cream sauce. *Cream Sauce.*— $\frac{1}{2}$ cup butter, beaten till very light, 1 cup sugar, $\frac{1}{2}$ cup cream. Set the dish in a basin of hot water and stir until it is all creamy ; it will only take a minute or two.

Batter Pudding.

1 egg, 1 cup milk, 2 teaspoonfuls cream tartar, 1 teaspoonful saleratus, flour enough as for cake. Quarter 4 or 5 apples, turn the batter over them, and bake an hour.

Delicate Pudding.

$\frac{1}{2}$ cup raw rice boiled in $1\frac{1}{2}$ cups of water. When it is nearly done add 2 cups of milk, and cook until the rice is soft. Add the yolks of 4 eggs beaten with $\frac{1}{2}$ cup of sugar, a little salt, and $\frac{1}{2}$ teaspoonful extract of vanilla. Take from the fire and stir in the beaten whites of two eggs. Make a meringue of the remaining whites beaten with $\frac{1}{2}$ cup of sugar. Spread over the top and set in the oven to brown.

Oxford Pudding.

Pare and quarter 4 large tart apples and boil in so little water that when done no water remains. Mash, and add 1 tablespoon-

IF . . .
YOU .
WANT

Success in Cooking, don't forget the

E. T. S. & CO.

Tin Boxes

SPICES.

———⟨⟨I⟩⟩———

They keep their strength.

As good next year as this.

ful melted butter, ½ cup sugar, (more if the apples are very sour), ½ cup of fine bread crumbs, the yolks of 4, and the whites of 2 eggs beaten light. Cover with a frosting made of the whites of 2 eggs and 1 cup of sugar. Bake until it is light brown.

Snow Pudding.

Soak half a box Plymouth Rock gelatine in half a cup of cold water two hours. Pour on to this nearly a pint of boiling water. Stir until the gelatine is dissolved, then add two cups sugar and the juice of 2 large lemons; stir this a few minutes, then add the whites of 6 eggs. Beat until it is white and stiff, then turn into molds and cool. *Sauce.*—Boil 1 pint of milk, add the beaten yolks of 6 eggs, and ½ cup of sugar. Salt, and flavor with vanilla. Serve ice cold.

Indian Pudding.

Take 1 quart of milk, pour all but 1 gill into a dish to scald. Mix a small cup of meal with the gill until smooth, and pour gradually into the boiling milk. Sweeten with molasses to taste (about a cupful). Add a little salt and cinnamon. Bake two or three hours. While baking, pour a tablespoonful of cold milk over the top, three or four times.

White Pudding Sauce.

1 cup milk, scald and thicken with 1 tablespoonful cornstarch, then add 1 cup of sugar and butter size of an egg beaten to a cream. Turn all over the beaten white of 1 egg just before serving. Flavor with vanilla or any other extract.

Snow Pudding.

¼ box of Nelson's gelatine, or ½ of Cox's, dissolved in 1 cup of cold water; pour on 1 cup boiling water, add while hot 1 good cup sugar and juice of 3 lemons; let cool, after straining. Stir occasionally, and before it hardens add whites of 3 eggs beaten stiff. Beat all until quite light; when nearly stiff enough to drop, pour into a mold. Serve with a soft custard made of the yolks.

PASTRY.

Frosted Lemon Pie.

2 eggs, 1 cup sugar, 1 cup boiling water, 1 teaspoonful corn starch. Cook in a double boiler. Save the white of one egg for frosting. This makes one pie. Line a plate with rich puff paste and when the filling is cool add the frost.

CHARLES D. THAYER,

Marlboro Pie.

1 pint sifted apple, 1 pint milk, 2 eggs, 2 tablespoonfuls melted butter, ½ wine glass of brandy or wine. Sweeten to your taste.

Marlboro Pie.

Pare, core, stew, and sift 6 apples. 6 eggs, 1 pint cream, ¼ lb. melted butter, sugar to taste, grated rind of 2 lemons, juice of 1.

Pastry.

3 cups flour, 1 cup lard, salt, ½ teaspoonful Royal baking powder, sifted with the flour. Very cold water. Handle as little as possible.

Cocoanut Pie.

Line a pie plate with crust (as for squash pie). Boil 1 pint milk and ½ cup Schepp's cocoanut together. When boiled add 1 teaspoonful butter, and 2 eggs beaten with ½ cup of sugar. Fill the plate and bake in a quick oven.

Cocoanut Pie.

1 pt. milk, ½ cup sugar, 2 eggs, a pinch of salt, butter the size of a walnut, ½ cup dessicated cocoanut. Bake with one crust.

Lemon Pie.

1 cup milk with 1 teaspoonful corn starch cooked in it, 1 cup sugar, juice and rind of 1 lemon, a little salt, 3 eggs; reserve the whites of 2 eggs for frosting. Cook the crust a little before putting in the custard. Frost with whites of eggs and 2 tablespoonfuls sugar.

Lemon Pie.

First bake pastry in pie plate. For the filling use 1 cup sugar. 1 cup boiling water, yolks of 2 eggs, 2 large tablespoonfuls corn starch. Mix beaten yolks, lemon juice and grated rind together. Pour on to it the sugar and boiling water mixed together. Put all into a dish on the stove and stir in the moistened cornstarch. Cook two or three minutes. When cool pour on to pastry. Beat whites of eggs for frosting, and add a little sugar and lemon extract.

Grandma's Pie.

One half cup raisins, 1 cup chopped rhubarb, 1 cup sugar, 1 egg, salt, small piece of butter.

Frosted Lemon Pie.

Juice and grated rind of 2 lemons, 1½ cups sugar, ¾ cup milk, yolks of 3 eggs, 2 tablespoonfuls flour. *Frosting.*—Whites 3 eggs, beaten stiff, 4 tablespoonfuls sugar.

Lemon Pie with Two Crusts.

The juice and grated rind of 1 lemon, 1 cup sugar, 1 egg, 1 spoonful flour, one-half cup milk or water.

Mock Mince Pie.

1 cup thick sour milk, 1 small cup sugar, 1½ cups of chopped raisins, 2 eggs, 1 small teaspoonful of spices. This will make two pies.

Raisin Pie.

1 cup raisins chopped and seeded, 1 cup cold water, 1 tablespoonful flour, piece of butter size of an egg. Bake with 2 crusts.

Chopped Paste.

Chop 1 cup butter, 1 pint flour, ½ teaspoonful salt, until it looks like Indian meal. Wet with ice water. Roll out and roll up like jelly roll. Put on ice until wanted.

Mock Mince Pie. (One pie.)

2½ common crackers, pounded fine, ½ cup boiling water, ½ cup molasses, ¼ cup butter, juice and grated rind of 1 large lemon, one-half cup chopped raisins. Add a little sugar if the lemons make it too tart, and spice to taste. Boil all together for about ten minutes.

Puffs.

NICE FOR PICNICS.

Make nice pie-crust for turnovers, and fill with the following mixture: 1 cup raisins stoned and chopped, 1 egg, 1 cup sugar, tiny pinch salt, juice and grated rind of 1 lemon.

CAKE.

Walnut Cake.

3 eggs, 2 cups sugar, 3 cups flour, 1 cup milk, ¾ cup butter, not quite a cupful of English walnuts, broken up, 3 even teaspoonfuls baking powder. Divide the frosting into small squares, laying half a nut in the middle of each square.

Filling for Washington Pie.

The juice and grated rind of 1 lemon, ½ cup sugar, ½ cup water. Boil sugar, water and lemon together, thicken with one dessert-spoonful corn-starch, and cook a few minutes.

Walnut Cake

1½ cups sugar, ½ cup butter, 3 eggs, 2½ cups flour, ½ cup milk, 1 teaspoonful cream of tartar, one-half teaspoonful saleratus, 1 cup nut meats chopped.

Corn Starch Cake.   .

Whites of 3 eggs, ½ cup corn starch, ½ cup butter, ½ cup milk, 1 cup sugar, 1 cup flour, one-half teaspoonful cream of tartar, one-quarter teaspoonful saleratus.

Cocoanut Loaf Cake.

1 cup butter, 1½ cups sugar, ¾ cup milk, 1 cup grated cocoanut, 2 cups flour, whites 4 eggs, 2 teaspoonfuls Royal baking powder.

Nut Cake.

⅔ cup sugar, ½ cup butter, ½ cup milk, 2 cups flour, 1 heaping teaspoonful Royal baking powder, 1 pound English walnuts, 1 pound raisins chopped, 3 eggs, little salt.

Marble Cake.

LIGHT PART.—1 cup sugar, ½ cup butter, ½ cup milk, 1 teaspoonful cream of tartar, one-half teaspoonful saleratus, whites of 3 eggs. One and one-half cups flour.

DARK PART.—1 cup sugar, ½ cup butter, ½ cup molasses, 2 cups flour, 1 teaspoonful cream of tartar, one-half teaspoonful saleratus, yolks of 3 eggs. Spice to taste.

Lemon Jelly Cake.

1½ cups sugar, ½ cup butter, ½ cup milk, 3 eggs, 2½ cups flour, 1 teaspoonful cream of tartar, one-half teaspoonful saleratus.

For the Jelly.—1 egg, juice of 1 lemon, two small apples grated.   Boil till thick as jelly.

Poor Man's Fruit Cake.

1½ cups brown sugar, 2 cups flour, 1 cup butter, 3 eggs, 1 cup chopped raisins, 3 tablespoonfuls sour milk, one-half teaspoonful soda, one-half cup blackberry jam.   Bake in a moderate oven.

Sponge Cake.

3 eggs, yolks and whites beaten separately, 1 cup sugar, 1½ cups flour, ½ teaspoonful soda, 1 teaspoonful cream of tartar, ½ cup cold water.   Flavor with vanilla.   Bake half an hour.

Raisin Cake.

One-half cup sugar, ¼ cup butter, ½ cup molasses, 2 eggs, 2 cups flour, 1 cup stoned raisins, ½ teaspoonful saleratus, clove, cinnamon and nutmeg.

Chocolate Cake.

2 cups sugar, 1 cup butter, 1 cup milk, 3 cups flour, yolks of 5 eggs and whites of 3, 1 teaspoonful yeast powder.   Bake in two layers.   *Frosting for Chocolate Cake.*— Beat the whites of 2 eggs with 1½ cups of powdered sugar.   Add 2 squares of chocolate and a little vanilla.

Boiled Frosting.

1 cup granulated sugar, ⅓ cup boiling water, white of 1 egg, 1 salt spoon cream of tartar.   Boil the sugar and water (without stirring) about 5 minutes, or until the syrup taken up will rope. Beat the egg stiff, add cream of tartar, and then pour the boiling syrup over the egg in a fine stream, beating it well.

Cream Cakes.

1 cup water (boiling), ½ cup butter, 3 eggs, pinch saleratus, 1 cup flour.   Stir the butter into the boiling water, then the flour. Stir until the mixture is stiff enough to drop from the spoon. Bake in a hot oven.   *Cream for filling.*—1 pint milk, 3 tablespoonfuls corn starch, ½ cup sugar, 1 egg.

Gingerbread.

1 cup sour milk, 1 cup molasses, ½ cup butter or lard, 2 eggs, 1 teaspoonful ginger, 1½ teaspoonfuls soda, flour enough to make as thick as pound cake.   Put ginger, butter and molasses together and make quite warm.

Spiced Gingerbread.

1 cup butter, ½ cup sugar, 1½ cups molasses, 1 cup sour milk, 3 eggs, 1½ teaspoonfuls soda, ½ teaspoonful of all kinds spice, 5 cups flour.

Nut Cake.

1½ cups sugar, ½ cup butter, 2 cups flour, ¾ cup milk, 1 teaspoonful cream of tartar, one-half teaspoonful soda, whites of 4 eggs, 1 cup nuts chopped. This makes 2 loaves, or 1 large one.

Ladies' Cake.

1 cup sugar, ½ cup butter, ½ cup milk, 2 cups flour, ½ teaspoonful soda, 1 teaspoonful saleratus, 1 teaspoonful extract almond, whites of 3 eggs, added last.

Chocolate Cake.

2 cups sugar, 4 eggs, ¾ cup of butter, ½ cup of milk, 2½ cups of flour, 1 teaspoonful cream of tartar, one-half teaspoonful soda, ½ cake of Baker's chocolate. Bake slowly. This makes 2 loaves.

Hot Water Sponge Cake.

6 eggs, 2 cups sugar, 2 cups pastry flour, ½ cup boiling water, grated rind of one-half lemon, and 1 teaspoonful juice. Beat yolks and sugar to a froth, add the lemon, then the boiling water, next the whites beaten stiff, and last the flour. Bake in two sheets in moderate oven half an hour.

Orange Cake.

2 cups sugar, 2 cups flour, ½ cup water, yolks of 5 eggs, whites of 3 eggs, one-half teaspoonful soda, 1 teaspoonful cream of tartar, juice and grated rind of 1 orange. Bake for layer cake.

Filling.—Whites of 2 eggs, 1 cup sugar, juice and grated rind of 1 orange.

Grandmother's Cake.

1 cup butter, 3 cups sugar, 5 eggs, 1 cup cream, 4 cups flour, raisins and spices to taste, one-half teaspoonful (small) of soda.

Fruit Cake.

4 coffee-cups flour, 3 coffee-cups sugar, 2 coffee-cups butter, 2 lbs. currants, ½ lb. citron, 1 nutmeg, 1 teaspoonful each cloves and cinnamon, 8 eggs, (whites and yolks beaten separately), 1 teaspoonful soda put in flour dry. This will make 2 loaves, baked in 2-quart tins. Bake two hours.

Peach Cream Pie.

3 eggs, 1 cup sugar, 1½ cups flour, 1 teaspoonful cream of tartar in the flour, 4 tablespoonfuls milk, one-half teaspoonful soda,

2 tablespoonfuls melted butter.   *Cream for Peach Pie.*—2 cups sifted peach, 2 cups cream whipped very stiff; stir the two together, flavor with 1 teaspoonful vanilla.   Sweeten to taste. Put layer between cake and on top.

Cheap Fruit Cake.

1 cup butter, 3 eggs, 2 cups sugar, 5 cups flour, 1 cup molasses, 1 cup milk, 2 cups raisins, a little citron, 1 teaspoonful all kinds of spice, 1 teaspoonful soda.   This makes two loaves.

Dayton Cake.

1 cup butter whipped to a cream, 2 cups sugar, add one at a time, 3 cups flour, ½ cup milk, 5 eggs, whites and yolks beaten separately, 1 teaspoonful baking powder.   Bake in 2 square tins. Frost 1 loaf with chocolate and to the other add a cup of fruit, and frost with white frosting.

White Cake.

1 cup sugar, ¼ cup butter, ½ cup milk, 1½ cups flour, 1 teaspoonful cream of tartar, ½ teaspoonful soda, whites of 2 eggs beaten to a froth.   Flavor.

Cocoanut Cake.

⅔ cup cocoanut soaked in ⅔ cup of milk fifteen minutes, ⅔ cup of sugar, 1 cup flour, 1 tablespoonful butter, 1 egg, 1 teaspoonful cream of tartar, 1 teaspoonful soda.

Dicolominie Cake.

1 cup butter, 2 cups sugar, 5 eggs, 3 cups flour, 2 teaspoonfuls baking powder, ½ lb. currants, ¼ citron cut fine, just a little nutmeg and cinnamon.

Gentlemen's Favorite Cake.

1½ cups sugar, ½ cup butter, 3 eggs, 2 teaspoonfuls cream of tartar, 1 teaspoonful soda in one-half cup milk, 2 cups flour.   Bake in 2 sheets.

Filling.—1 egg, 1 cup sugar, 3 grated apples, juice of 1 lemon and just a little grated peel.   Mix and cook over teakettle until it becomes thick.   Let it cool before putting in cake.   Frost the top with boiled frosting.

Boiled Frosting for Cake.

1 cup granulated sugar, ¼ cup boiling water.   Boil gently until the mixture strings, (about 4 minutes).   Pour slowly upon the white of 1 egg, beaten to a froth.   Flavor with vanilla.

Cup Cake.

1½ cups sugar, ½ cup butter, ½ cup milk, 2 cups flour, 4 eggs, 1 teaspoonful yeast powder.

Chocolate Cake.
1 cup sugar, ½ cup butter, ½ cup milk, 1 cup flour, 2 eggs, ½ teaspoonful saleratus, 1 teaspoonful cream tartar, 2 squares chocolate (Baker's). Melt the chocolate and stir into butter and sugar.

White Cake.
1½ cups sugar, ½ cup of butter, 1 cup milk (scant), 2½ cups flour, with 3 tablespoonfuls corn starch, and 2 teaspoonfuls baking powder sifted 4 times. Lastly, add whites of 4 eggs beaten stiff.

Sour Milk Cake.
1½ cups sugar, ½ cup butter, ½ cup sour milk, ½ teaspoonful saleratus, 1½ cups flour, juice of half a lemon, yolks of 3, whites of 2 eggs.

Spice Cake.
1 cup butter, ½ cup sugar, 2 eggs, 1 teaspoonful saleratus in one-half cup of milk, 2 cups flour, ½ teaspoonful each of cloves, cinnamon and nutmeg, 1 cup raisins.

Sponge Cake.
1 even tumblerful sugar, 1 heaping tumblerful flour, 5 eggs, beaten separately, 1 teaspoonful cream of tartar, ½ teaspoonful saleratus.

Sour Milk Spice Cake.
1 cup sour milk, 1 cup sugar, ½ cup butter, 2 cups flour, 1 egg, 1 teaspoonful saleratus, ½ cup chopped raisins, 1 teaspoonful cinnamon, ¼ teaspoonful clove, ¼ teaspoonful mace.

Dayton Cake.
1 cup butter, 2 cups sugar, 3 cups flour, ½ cup milk, 1 teaspoonful cream of tartar, ½ teaspoonful saleratus, 5 eggs.

Fruit Cake.
1 cup butter, 2 cups sugar, 3 cups flour (heaping), 1 cup milk, scant teaspoonful saleratus, raisins, currants, and citron to fill a large cup, a little nutmeg, large spoonful of brandy.

Cup Cake.
1 cup sugar, 2 eggs, ½ cup butter, 1½ cups flour, ¼ cup milk, ¼ teaspoonful soda, cinnamon, nutmeg, and salt, 1 cup of raisins, stoned and chopped.

Cocoanut Cake.
1 cup sugar, ½ cup butter, ½ cup milk, 1 cup cocoanut, 1½ cups flour, 3 eggs, 1 teaspoonful cream tartar, ½ teaspoonful saleratus.

Lemon Cake.
1 lb. of sugar, 1 lb. flour, ½ lb. butter, 7 eggs, grated rind and juice of 2 lemons, 1 tumbler currants, saleratus as big as a pea. Will make two loaves.

Dried Apple Cake.

2 cups dried apple soaked over night, then chopped and simmered 3 hours in 1½ cups molasses, 2 cups milk, 2 eggs, 2 teaspoonfuls saleratus, spice of all kinds, salt, 5 cups flour, 2 cups sugar, 1 cup butter. This makes 2 loaves.

Railroad Cake.

1 cup sugar, 3 eggs, 3 tablespoonfuls melted butter, 3 tablespoonfuls milk, ¼ teaspoonful soda, ½ teaspoonful cream of tartar, 2 cups flour. Use lemon or other flavoring.

Cocoanut Cream.

Cake Filling.—1 cup raisins stoned and chopped fine, ½ cup chopped almonds, ½ cup grated cocoanut, white of 1 egg beaten stiff.

COOKIES.

Sour Cream Cookies.

1 cup rich sour cream, 1 cup sugar, salt, 1 teaspoonful saleratus, flour enough to roll thin. Bake in a quick oven.

Molasses Cookies.

1 cup molasses, 1 cup sugar, 1 cup hot water, ½ cup butter, 1 dessert-spoonful saleratus, ½ teaspoonful each ginger and cinnamon. Mix soft enough to drop on buttered tin. Quick oven.

Sugar Cookies.

2 cups sugar, 1 cup butter, 2 eggs, ½ cup cold water, ½ teaspoonful saleratus, flour. Roll very thin.

Ginger Snaps.

1 cup molasses, 1 cup sugar, 1 cup butter or drippings. Melt all together, and pour on to 1 qt. flour. Dissolve 1 teaspoonful saleratus in a large spoonful of vinegar, ½ teaspoonful each of ginger and cinnamon. Add flour enough to mix quite stiff. Roll very thin.

Sugar Cookies. (Very nice).

½ cup butter, 1 cup sugar, ¼ cup milk, 1 egg, 2 even teaspoonfuls baking powder. Flour to roll out thin. Cream the butter and sugar, add the egg, well beaten, the milk and baking powder, mixed with 2 cups of flour, then enough more flour to roll out. By adding 1 cup grated cocoanut a nice cookie is made.

Cookies.

2 cups sugar, 1 cup butter, 3 eggs, 4 tablespoonfuls water, 1 teaspoonful soda. Roll out thin and bake immediately.

Drop Cookies.

1 cup sugar, ½ cup butter, 2 eggs, 2 cups flour, 2 large table-spoonfuls milk, 2 heaping teaspoonfuls baking powder. Drop a teaspoonful on buttered tins. If liked, sprinkle sugar on top and flavor.

DOUGHNUTS, FRITTERS, &c.

Buckwheat Griddle-cakes.

3 cups buckwheat, 1½ cups flour, 1 quart tepid water, ½ compressed yeast-cake. In the morning, just before frying, add ¼ teaspoonful saleratus.

Plain Griddle-cakes,

Make a thin batter over night with white flour, 1 qt. milk, 1 egg, one-half yeast cake. Add a little saleratus and salt just before frying. Very nice.

Rye Drop-cakes.

1 cup rye, 1 cup Indian meal, 1 egg, 1 cup flour, small teaspoonful soda, milk to mix soft. Drop from spoon into hot fat.

Good Raised Doughnuts.

1 egg, 1 cup sugar, 3 tablespoonfuls butter, 3 tablespoofuls home made yeast, 1 cup milk, spice, nutmeg, etc.

English Puffs.

Boil 1 pint of milk, and while it is boiling stir in flour enough for the spoon to stand up in the batter. When cold, add ½ a tablespoonful melted butter, a little salt, and 6 eggs, one at a time without beating. Drop from a spoon into hot lard (or cottolene) and fry a light brown. Sprinkle sugar over them as soon as they are taken from the fat, and serve at once, without sauce.

Pancakes.

1½ pints sour milk, 3 eggs, 2 teaspoonfuls saleratus, 1½ cups molasses. Mix hard enough to drop in the hot fat with half rye and half Indian meal, and salt. *Hot* fat or poor cakes.

Corn Fritters.

2 cups grated corn, 2 crackers rolled fine, 2 eggs, whites and yolks beaten separately. Fry like oysters. Canned corn can be used as well if put through a meat chopper, 1 can making 2 cups of corn.

Apple Fritters.

2 eggs, 1 teaspoonful melted butter, 1 cup milk, 2 teaspoonfuls baking powder, 1 teaspoonful soda, enough flour for a stiff

batter.   Pare apples, core and slice them and mix with batter, and fry slowly in hot fat.   When done sprinkle with sugar. Serve hot.

Doughnuts.

1 cup sugar, 2 eggs, 1 cup milk, 2 small teaspoonfuls cream of tartar, 1 small teaspoonful saleratus.   If the milk is not rich, add a little melted butter; salt and a little cinnamon.   Mix quite soft with Haxall flour.

Doughnuts.

1 coffee-cup sweet milk, 2 eggs, butter size of a walnut, 2 heaping teaspoonfuls Royal baking powder, cinnamon or nutmeg to taste.   Fry in hot lard or cottolene, turning frequently.   Have the dough as soft as can be handled.

Doughnuts.

1 cup sugar, 1 egg, $\frac{2}{3}$ cup sour milk, 1 teaspoonful cream of tartar, 1 teaspoonful soda, a little salt and nutmeg, flour enough to mix soft.

PRESERVES.

Tomato Preserves.

3 lbs. of tomato peeled and cut, the juice and grated rind of 2 lemons.   Cook all together 1 hour, then add 4 lbs. sugar, some pieces of ginger root, and boil about half an hour, or until the sauce is clear and nearly jellied.   This is very nice.

Grape Jelly.

Heat and crush the grapes in a kettle and cook until done; then drain through a sieve, but not press through.   To each pt. of juice allow 1 lb. of heated sugar.   Boil rapidly 5 minutes, then add sugar and boil 3 minutes longer.

Brandy Peaches.

1 lb. peaches, $\frac{1}{2}$ pound sugar.   Dissolve the sugar in a little water.   Put in your peaches, and when you can push a broom corn through them easily, take them off the fire and let them cool.   Let the syrup cool, and add as much brandy as syrup. Seal them up tight.

Preserved Pears.

8 pounds sliced pears, 4 pounds granulated sugar, 1 oz. white ginger root, 4 sliced lemons.   Soak ingredients together over night.   Boil till clear.

Pickled Peaches.

Make syrup of 1 qt. vinegar and 6 lbs. sugar. Boil and skim, then add 1 ounce whole cloves. Pare 1 peck of ripe but not soft fruit. Boil in syrup till tender. This fills 6 quart jars.

Apple Ginger.

4 lbs. each of apples and sugar. Make a syrup of the sugar with a pint of water. Chop the apples very fine, with one oz. green ginger, or, if you cannot get that, use white ginger root. Put in the syrup with the grated rind of four lemons, and boil slowly 2 hours or until it looks clear.

Spiced Rhubarb. (Good.)

Peel and slice the rhubarb and weigh it. Put it in a porcelain kettle, and place where it will heat gradually until the juice flows freely. Bring forward on the stove and boil gently half an hour. Dip out half the juice and keep warm. Add to the cooked fruit $\frac{1}{2}$ lb. sugar for each lb. of rhubarb used, and also to each pound allow 1 teaspoonful cloves, and 2 cinnamon. If too thick, reduce with the warm juice. It should not be quite so thick as jam. Simmer for ten minutes and pour into glass jars. When cool, wrap each jar in thick paper. Keep in cool, dry place.

To Can Corn.

To 8 pints of cut corn add 3 pints of water and boil 20 minutes. Then add $\frac{3}{4}$ of a pint of table salt, and boil two or three minutes. Can immediately while boiling. It will keep a long time in glass cans. Sweet corn is the best. To prepare it soak or wash thoroughly till all the brine is out. Then season with butter, milk and pepper.

CONFECTIONS.

Kisses.

Beat the whites of 3 fresh eggs to a stiff froth, add 6 tablespoonfuls powdered sugar. Flavor with vanilla. Have ready a buttered pan, in which to lay a white paper, drop on with a teaspoon, and sift granulated sugar over them. Bake in a slow oven half an hour.

Glace Nuts and Fruits.

Boil 2 cups sugar and 1 cup of boiling water till it threads. Add $\frac{1}{2}$ cup vinegar, and boil until when tried in ice water it will crack between the teeth. With buttered forks dip the nuts or fruit into the syrup, and drop on to buttered tins.

Candy.

2 cups sugar, ½ cup water, 2 teaspoonfuls vinegar, piece of butter the size of an egg. Don't stir after it melts. Pour in buttered pans, and cut in squares.

Butter Scotch.

2 cups brown sugar, 1 cup water, 2 even tablespoonfuls butter. Boil sugar and water till hard enough to break when tried in water; then add melted butter, and pour into a buttered dish. Do not stir while cooking.

Chocolate Creams.

Melt one square unsweetened chocolate with 1 teaspoonful water, add an equal quantity melted fondant, and in this mixture dip white balls of fondant flavored with vanilla. Cool on buttered paper. Be careful not to let the chocolate cook; it must melt only, and it is better to put it in a dish over the steam of the tea-kettle. To prepare the fondant.—Boil 2 cups granulated sugar and 1 scant cup boiling water, till it threads, when it can be gathered in a soft ball when dropped in ice water. When lukewarm, beat until thick enough to knead; work until smooth; knead in the hands by squeezing, pressing and rolling, till it looks and feels much like lard. Fondant makes an excellent frosting. A layer of chocolate over it makes a chocolate cream frosting which is delicious.

Chocolate Caramels.

1 cup sugar, 1 cup molasses, 1 cup chocolate, grated, 1 cup milk, ½ cup butter, 1 teaspoonful vanilla. Boil briskly for 20 minutes. Pour in buttered pans; when cool mark off in squares.

Chocolate Caramels.

5 scant cups granulated sugar, ½ lb. unsweetened chocolate, 1 cup cream or milk, and 3 tablespoonfuls butter. Boil all together twenty minutes, stirring meanwhile, then try in cold water; if it will crack it is done. If cooked a little longer it will be sugary.

Cream Peppermints.

Boil 2 cups granulated sugar and ½ cup boiling water five minutes. Add a few drops oil of peppermint. Beat to a cream, and drop on buttered paper.

Checkermints are made in the same way, only colored pink with cochineal, and flavored with wintergreen.

For Chocolatemints, add a few drops of melted chocolate to the boiled sugar and water and flavor with vanilla.

Easy Candy.

The white of an egg, an equal quantity of water and confectioners' sugar. Put between walnuts, dates, etc.

Nut Meringues.

Beat whites of 3 eggs to a froth, add 1 saltspoonful cream of tartar, and continue beating until stiff. Add ¾ cupful powdered sugar and ¼ cupful chopped walnuts. Drop on buttered paper and bake in a very slow oven 30 minutes.

TABLE OF WEIGHTS AND MEASURES.

16 Tablespoonfuls of liquid = 1 Cup.
12 Tablespoonfuls of dry material = 1 Cup.
4 Cups of liquid = 1 Quart.
4 Cups of flour = 1 Pound or 1 Quart.
2 Cups of solid butter = 1 Pound.
2 Cups of granulated sugar = 1 Pound.
2½ Cups of powdered sugar = 1 Pound.
3 Cups of meal = 1 Pound.
1 Pint of milk or water = 1 Pound.
1 Pint of chopped meat packed solidly = 1 Pound.
9 Large eggs or 10 medium eggs = 1 Pound.
1 Round tablespoonful butter = 1 Ounce.
1 Tablespoonful of liquid = ½ Ounce.
2 Round tablespoonfuls of flour = 1 Ounce.
2 Round tablespoonfuls of sugar = 1 Ounce.

TIME TO COOK MEATS, VEGETABLES, ETC.

Beef Sirloin, Rare.— Eight minutes for each pound.
Beef Sirloin, Well done.—Ten to fifteen minutes for each pound.
Lamb, Well done.— Fifteen minutes for each pound.
Mutton, Rare.—Ten to twelve minutes.
Mutton, Well done.—Fifteen to eighteen minutes.
Pork, Well done.—Twenty-five to thirty minutes.
Veal, Well done.— Eighteen to twenty minutes.

4

Chicken, weighing from three to five pounds.—One and one-half hours.
Turkeys, weighing from nine to twelve pounds.—Three and one-half hours.
Fish of average thickness, weighing from six to eight pounds.— One hour.
Plain Cake.—Twenty to forty-five minutes.
Cookies.—Ten to twelve minutes.
Plum Pudding.—Three hours.
Pies with two crusts.—Thirty to forty minutes.
Bread.—Forty to sixty minutes.
Biscuit.—Ten to eighteen minutes.
String Beans.—One and a half to two hours, in cold water.
Shell Beans.—One to two hours, in cold water.
Corn.—Twenty to thirty minutes, in boiling water.
Asparagus.—Fifteen to eighteen minutes in boiling salted water.
Peas.—Fifteen to twenty minutes, in cold water.
Potatoes.—Twenty to thirty minutes, in boiling water.
Cauliflower.—Thirty to forty minutes.
Cabbage.—Thirty to forty-five minutes.

DIRECTIONS FOR RESTORING PERSONS APPARENTLY DEAD FROM DROWNING.

Loosen all tight articles of clothing about the neck and chest. Remove the froth and mucus from the mouth and nostrils. Hold the body, *for a few seconds only*, with the head hanging down, so that the water may run out of the lungs and windpipe. See that the tongue is pulled forward if it falls back into the throat. By taking hold of it with a handkerchief it will not slip.

If breathing has ceased, or nearly so, it must be stimulated by pressure of the chest with the hands, in imitation of the natural breathing, forcibly expelling the air from the lungs and allowing it to re-enter and expand them by the elasticity of the ribs. This is the *most important step of all.* To do it readily, lay the person on his back with a cushion or some firm substance under his shoulders; then press with the flat of the hands over the lower part of the breast bone and the upper part of the abdomen, keeping up a regular repetition and relaxation of pressure twenty or thirty times a minute. A pressure of thirty pounds may be applied with safety to a grown person.

Rub the limbs with the hands or dry cloths constantly, to aid the circulation and keep the body warm. As soon as the person can swallow, give warm drink.

EMERGENCIES.

What shall we do before the Doctor arrives?

In the limited space the compiler of this useful little book has allowed me, I shall confine myself to suggestions on those diseases which frequently occur, the first and second in infancy and childhood, the latter in most cases between the ages of fifty and seventy.

There is probably no disease that so strikes terror to the heart of father and mother as croup. It often comes on suddenly with hoarseness and a short dry cough, which soon grows metallic or "brassy," and the difficulty of breathing quickly increases and is most distressing, the child seeming to fight for breath and to require all its strength to force the air in and out of its chest. The face is flushed, and the voice and breathing make a peculiar sound, which once heard is never forgotten.

Keep the child in a warm room and apply hot water compresses to the throat, changing them every ten minutes until medical aid arrives. Spasmodic croup is usually relieved in a short time. Membranous croup is of much more rare occurrence, but often fatal.

Convulsions is another disease which has usually a sudden onset, and is alarming to both family and physician. When convulsions occur send for a doctor at once. In the meantime seek to learn the cause of the attack, whether from disordered dentition, whooping cough, or indigestible matter in the stomach. If the latter, give the patient something to throw it off. Strong salt and water is usually effective, or add a little mustard to the water. If the child is feverish, put it in a hot bath, temperature of 100 degrees Fahrenheit. Do not trust to your hand to judge of the warmth of the water, lest in your haste and excitement you may put the child into too hot water, and scald the unconscious little patient. That very thing has been done.

While the child is in the bath, place a sponge or cloth wet in cold water on its head. The bath should last from ten minutes to half an hour. Then wrap the little one in warm flannel, and if the head is still hot, continue the cold applications. It is hoped by this time the physician has arrived to assume the burden of responsibility in the case.

Apoplexy is another grave disease which is accompanied with sudden loss of sense and motion, though the mechanical action of the heart and lungs still continues. A person attacked falls suddenly and lies without moving. Unconsciousness is usually complete for some seconds, minutes or hours. During the coma the breathing is commonly stertorous, and the pulse slow and full, the head hot, and the face more or less dark or flushed.

The most that can be done until the doctor comes is to place the patient in a semi-prone position, so the head will be raised. Relieve tension of all bands about the throat, chest and abdomen, and apply cold compresses to the head.

In all emergencies remember that common sense, combined with a clear, cool head, is of the first importance in both nurse and medical attendant. Little does it matter how great our knowledge if we cannot make good use of it when needed.

REMEDIES AND HEALTH HINTS.

For dust in the eyes avoid rubbing; dash water into them.

Remove cinders, etc., with the round point of a lead pencil.

If an artery is cut, compress above the wound; if a vein is cut, compress below.

If choked, get upon all fours and cough.

For light burns dip the part in cold water; if the skin is destroyed, cover with varnish.

Smother a fire with carpets; water will often spread burning oil, and increase the danger.

Before passing through smoke, take a full breath, and then stoop low; but if carbon is suspected, walk erect.

Suck poison wounds, unless your mouth is sore, enlarge the wound, or, better, cut out the part without delay.   Hold the wounded part as long as can be borne to a hot coal or the end of a cigar.

For apoplexy, raise the head and body; for fainting, lay the person flat.

CULINARY HINTS.

There is a greenness in onions and potatoes that renders them hard to digest.   For health's sake put them in warm water for an hour before cooking.

Single cream is cream that has stood on the milk twelve hours.   It is best for tea and coffee.   Double cream stands on its milk twenty-four hours, and cream for butter frequently stands forty-eight hours.   Cream that is to be whipped should not be butter cream, lest in whipping it change to butter.

The only kind of stove with which you can preserve a uniform heat is a gas stove; with it you can simmer a pot for an hour, or boil at the same rate.

To beat the whites of eggs quickly, put in a pinch of salt. The cooler the eggs the quicker they will froth.

In boiling eggs, put them in boiling water ten minutes and then put them in cold water. This will prevent the yolks from turning black.

In making any sauce, put the butter and flour in together, and your sauce will never be lumpy.

Tepid water is produced by combining two-thirds cold and one-third boiling water.

To make macaroni tender, put it in cold water and bring to a boil.

Old potatoes may be freshened by plunging them into cold water before cooking them.

USEFUL HINTS.

Never leave the cover off the tea canister.

Clean piano keys with a soft cloth dipped in alcohol.

Egg stains on silver can be removed with table salt and a wet cloth.

Leather chair seats may be revived by rubbing them with well beaten white of egg.

Salts of lemon will take spots out of linen, and also remove stains from wood.

Never wash bronzed lamps, chandeliers, etc. Dust them with a soft woolen cloth.

A very thin coat of what is known as French picture varnish will restore chromos and oil paintings to their original brightness.

Hold a hot shovel over furniture to remove white spots.

Salt dissolved in alcohol will remove grease spots from cloth.

To extract ink from wood, scour with sand wet with water and ammonia, then rinse with strong saleratus water.

Mildew can be removed by soaking in buttermilk, or putting lemon juice and salt upon it and exposing it to the hot sun.

Take a bucket of fresh water into your bedroom every night, and let it remain uncovered. It will absorb all poisonous gases.

Paint stains that are dry and old may be removed from cotton or woolen goods with chloroform. First cover the spot with olive oil or butter.

Zinc is best cleaned with hot, soapy water, then polished with kerosene.

It is well to keep large pieces of charcoal in damp corners and dark places.

If the hands are rubbed on a stick of celery after peeling onions, the odor will be entirely removed.

Chloride of lime should be scattered at least once a week under sinks and in all places where sewer gas is liable to lurk.

The white of an egg is said to be a specific for fish bones sticking in the throat.   It is to be swallowed whole, and will carry down a bone easily.

The metallic tops of kerosene lamps can be cleaned by soaking in water in which beans have been boiled.

INDEX.